SHAKESPEARE ON
Fairies & Magic

SHAKESPEARE ON
Fairies & Magic

COMPILED BY

BENJAMIN DARLING

PRENTICE HALL PRESS

PRINTED IN SINGAPORE

10   9   8   7   6   5   4   3   2   1

ISBN   0-7352-0292-3

PRENTICE HALL PRESS
Paramus, NJ 07652

http://www.phdirect.com

FOREWORD

Illustrating Shakespeare

The better known a book, the more daunting is the challenge of illustrating it. Familiar stories and characters are like old friends. We know them, and are offended or disappointed of someone represents them contrary to our imagining. I, who have read the novels of Charles Dickens many times, cannot read with pleasure an edition illustrated by Phiz. Further, the works we esteem highest are the most difficult to illustrate, because the people and scenes have already achieved intense reality. What chance then has an illustrator with the works of Shakespeare, the most familiar and most sublimely successful of English writers? Can any envisioning be as lovely and fragile as the Ophelia we know? Does a picture of Lady Macbeth show a woman as ferocious as Shakespeare's? Can a picture of Falstaff be as grossly endearing as the one we have made of words? Yet, much wonderful work has been done despite these obstacles. Hundreds of portraits of Ophelia have been made, and though many are simply young women pretending to be this tragic heroine, some do live and show us things we hadn't known of her madness and beauty.

This volume wisely focuses on that area in which success is most probable — the fantastic. Even Shakespeare's ghosts and fairies are evocations rather than detailed portraits. This opens the door for painters and illustrators to rush in, and they have done so plentifully and with great skill. In my view the fantastic realm is the richest vein of Shakespearean illustration, and many of the pictures included here are by masters of imaginative illustration.

Welleran Poltarnees

INTRODUCTION

Fairies, ghosts, witches, magicians, elves and sprites, spells, incantations, visitations and charms; all of these supernatural creatures and events are found in abundance in the works of William Shakespeare. Almost every play has some mention of magic and a number of them are wholly concerned with it. Such interest in the supernatural realm is not unusual for writers of Shakespeare's day, but, as in everything else he touched, Shakespeare changed details where he saw fit and made up characters and characteristics when existing mythology was insufficient to his needs. In so doing he acted as a sorcerer of language who, through his charmed rhymes, has delighted and influenced every generation of writers and readers.

Fairies seemed to be of particular interest to Shakespeare; *A Midsummer Night's Dream* is devoted almost entirely to their activities. T.F. Thistleton Dyer in his excellent *Folk-Lore of Shakespeare* describes his fairy writing perfectly, "The wealth of Shakespeare's luxuriant imagination and glowing language seems to have been poured forth in the graphic accounts he has given us of the fairy tribe. Indeed, the profusion of poetic imagery with which he has so richly clad his fairy characters is unrivaled, and the *Midsummer Night's Dream* holds a unique position in so far as it contains the finest modern artistic realization of the fairy realm." The fairies of *A Midsummer Night's Dream* are quite different from the standard Elizabethan view which saw them as malicious little people about the size of a small child, bent on upsetting the activities of man and being a general nuisance. Shakespeare's fairies inhabit a kingdom of their own, complete with a royal family in Oberon and Titania. Shakespeare's fairies did meddle in the affairs of humans but they also had a life and concerns of their own far away from Elizabethan England. Shakespeare's fairies are also much smaller than the child sized Elizabethan fairy; they could fit easily into an acorn cup and are in constant danger of being drowned by the burst honey bags of bees. It is from this wonderful concept of tiny regal beings inhabiting their own kingdom, like the gods and goddesses of Athens that we take our modern view of fairies. Helen Hinton Stewart in *The Supernatural In Shakespeare* states emphatically, "If we think of fairies in the modern sense as beautiful or grotesque little beings of human form, dancing on the green-sward and hiding in the flowers; or speeding through the air on some benevolent or, it may be, mischievous errand...they are the creation of Shakespeare."

INTRODUCTION

Ghosts appear in many of Shakespeare's plays, *Julius Caesar*, *Macbeth* and *Hamlet* most prominently. Are they the products of imagination, as seems suggested in *Macbeth?* Or are they apparitions from beyond the grave? Banquo's confrontation with Macbeth over dinner seems to be Macbeth's own guilty conscience and waning sanity playing tricks upon him (and yet the witches seem real). On the other hand Hamlet's father's ghost is seen by a number of characters in the play and seems as real, if less corporeal, as anyone else in the play. Belief in ghosts was common in Elizabethan times, Bacon advises in *Advancement of Learning*, "The conversing with them or employment of them is prohibited, much more any veneration towards them." Shakespeare, typically, plays both sides of the question. At times he seems the modern skeptic, and at others the superstitious believer; he offers both arguments for our consideration.

Witches are one of the most enduring and believed creatures of the supernatural realm. In Shakespeare's time, as in early American history, witches were sought out and tried for their crimes. Their confessions made for hair-raising reading and would have provided rich fodder for any writer. Elizabethan witches were believed to have powers over the winds, some even sold the promise of fair winds to sailors. They could sail through the air and vanish at will. They possessed a variety of spells and charms, through which they could torture and ruin a man, as they did Macbeth. The witches in *Macbeth* are Scottish hags and Mr. Gunyon in his *Illustrations of Scottish History, Life and Superstition*, describes them thus, "They are hellish monsters, brewing hell-broth, having cats and toads for familiars, loving midnight, riding on the passing storm, and devilish evil against such as offend them. They crouch beneath the gibbet of the murderer, meet in gloomy caverns, amid earthquake convulsions, or in thunder, lightning and rain."

Magicians are human beings who have through study and practice, usually with the help of ancient and rare books of spells and magic, mastered the command of the natural and supernatural worlds. Prospero, in *The Tempest*, is one such magician who, when enrobed in his magical cloak, can command storms and other natural phenomena and has power over other creatures such as Ariel, the sprite, and Caliban, the witch Sycorax's son. It is often said that of all his characters Shakespeare put himself most fully into the character of Prospero who tells us:

INTRODUCTION

Our revels now are ended. These our actors,
As I foretold you, were all spirits, and
Are melted into air, into thin air;
And like the baseless fabric of this vision,
The cloud-capped towers, the gorgeous palaces,
The solemn temples, the great globe itself,
Yea, all which it inherit, shall dissolve;
And, like this insubstantial pageant faded,
Leave not a rack behind. We are such stuff
As dreams are made on...

The Tempest is one of Shakespeare's last plays and many have suggested that these words are a commentary on his own art and leave taking.

Sprites are spirits; they do not have bodies as fairies do. Ariel is a sprite and elves are a different, more workaday type of sprite, Sir Walter Scott referred to them as "Sprites of a coarser sort." Among the sprites Robin Goodfellow, or Puck, holds a special place. Robin Goodfellow was a native British sprite and would have been well known to every Englishman. Minor White Latham in *The Elizabethan Fairies* explains his position in folk legend, "Of all the spirits and terrors of the night, he was never known to possessor to make use of any supernatural powers fatal to mankind. Finally, he occupied the unique position of national practical joker whose presence furnished an excuse for any untoward domestic accident and connoted every mad prank and merry jest that could be devised." It is this harmless prankster that leads us through the delightful twists and turns of *A Midsummer Night's Dream*, and offers us this excellent advice at the end:

If we shadows have offended,
Think but this, and all is mended:
That you have but slumbered here,
While these visions did appear...

FAIRY

EITHER I MISTAKE YOUR SHAPE AND MAKING QUITE,

OR ELSE YOU ARE THAT SHREWD AND KNAVISH SPRITE

CALL'D ROBIN GOODFELLOW: ARE NOT YOU HE

THAT FRIGHTS THE MAIDENS OF THE VILLAGERY;

SKIM MILK, AND SOMETIMES LABOUR IN THE QUERN

AND BOOTLESS MAKE THE BREATHLESS HOUSEWIFE CHURN;

AND SOMETIME MAKE THE DRINK TO BEAR NO BARM;

MISLEAD NIGHT-WANDERERS, LAUGHING AT THEIR HARM?

THOSE THAT HOBGOBLIN CALL YOU AND SWEET PUCK,

YOU DO THEIR WORK, AND THEY SHALL HAVE GOOD LUCK:

ARE NOT YOU HE?

PUCK

THOU SPEAK'ST ARIGHT;
I AM THAT MERRY WANDERER OF THE NIGHT.
I JEST TO OBERON AND MAKE HIM SMILE
WHEN I A FAT AND BEAN-FED HORSE BEGUILE,
NEIGHING IN LIKENESS OF A FILLY FOAL:
AND SOMETIME LURK I IN A GOSSIP'S BOWL,
IN VERY LIKENESS OF A ROASTED CRAB,
AND WHEN SHE DRINKS, AGAINST HER LIPS I BOB
AND ON HER WITHER'D DEWLAP POUR THE ALE.
THE WISEST AUNT, TELLING THE SADDEST TALE,
SOMETIME FOR THREE-FOOT STOOL MISTAKETH ME;
THEN SLIP I FROM HER BUM, DOWN TOPPLES SHE,
AND 'TAILOR' CRIES, AND FALLS INTO A COUGH;
AND THEN THE WHOLE QUIRE HOLD THEIR HIPS AND LAUGH,
AND WAXEN IN THEIR MIRTH AND SNEEZE AND SWEAR
A MERRIER HOUR WAS NEVER WASTED THERE.
BUT, ROOM, FAIRY HERE COMES OBERON.

MISTRESS QUICKLY

FAIRIES, BLACK, GREY, GREEN, AND WHITE,

YOU MOONSHINE REVELLERS AND SHADES OF NIGHT,

YOU ORPHAN HEIRS OF FIXED DESTINY,

ATTEND YOUR OFFICE AND YOUR QUALITY.

CRIER HOBGOBLIN, MAKE THE FAIRY OYES.

ARIEL SINGS

FULL FATHOM FIVE THY FATHER LIES;

OF HIS BONES ARE CORAL MADE;

THOSE ARE PEARLS THAT WERE HIS EYES:

NOTHING OF HIM THAT DOTH FADE

BUT DOTH SUFFER A SEA-CHANGE

INTO SOMETHING RICH AND STRANGE.

SEA-NYMPHS HOURLY RING HIS KNELL

CALIBAN

BE NOT AFEARD; THE ISLE IS FULL OF NOISES,

SOUNDS AND SWEET AIRS, THAT GIVE DELIGHT AND HURT NOT.

SOMETIMES A THOUSAND TWANGLING INSTRUMENTS

WILL HUM ABOUT MINE EARS, AND SOMETIME VOICES

THAT, IF I THEN HAD WAKED AFTER LONG SLEEP,

WILL MAKE ME SLEEP AGAIN: AND THEN, IN DREAMING,

THE CLOUDS METHOUGHT WOULD OPEN AND SHOW RICHES

READY TO DROP UPON ME THAT, WHEN I WAKED,

I CRIED TO DREAM AGAIN.

ACT III SCENE II

PUCK

CAPTAIN OF OUR FAIRY BAND,
HELENA IS HERE AT HAND;
AND THE YOUTH, MISTOOK BY ME,
PLEADING FOR A LOVER'S FEE.
SHALL WE THEIR FOND PAGEANT SEE?
LORD, WHAT FOOLS THESE MORTALS BE!

ACT III SCENE II

OBERON

TAKE THOU SOME OF IT, AND SEEK THROUGH THIS GROVE:

A SWEET ATHENIAN LADY IS IN LOVE

WITH A DISDAINFUL YOUTH: ANOINT HIS EYES;

BUT DO IT WHEN THE NEXT THING HE ESPIES

MAY BE THE LADY: THOU SHALT KNOW THE MAN

BY THE ATHENIAN GARMENTS HE HATH ON.

EFFECT IT WITH SOME CARE, THAT HE MAY PROVE

MORE FOND ON HER THAN SHE UPON HER LOVE...

MACBETH

BANQUO

...WHAT ARE THESE
SO WITHER'D AND SO WILD IN THEIR ATTIRE,
THAT LOOK NOT LIKE THE INHABITANTS O' THE EARTH,
AND YET ARE ON'T? LIVE YOU? OR ARE YOU AUGHT
THAT MAN MAY QUESTION? YOU SEEM TO UNDERSTAND ME,
BY EACH AT ONCE HER CHAPPY FINGER LAYING
UPON HER SKINNY LIPS: YOU SHOULD BE WOMEN,
AND YET YOUR BEARDS FORBID ME TO INTERPRET
THAT YOU ARE SO.

HAMLET

COME HITHER, GENTLEMEN,
AND LAY YOUR HANDS AGAIN UPON MY SWORD:
NEVER TO SPEAK OF THIS THAT YOU HAVE HEARD,
SWEAR BY MY SWORD.

GHOST

SWEAR.

HAMLET

WELL SAID, OLD MOLE! CANST WORK I' THE EARTH SO FAST?
A WORTHY PIONER! ONCE MORE REMOVE, GOOD FRIENDS.

HORATIO

O DAY AND NIGHT, BUT THIS IS WONDROUS STRANGE!

HAMLET

AND THEREFORE AS A STRANGER GIVE IT WELCOME.
THERE ARE MORE THINGS IN HEAVEN AND EARTH, HORATIO,
THAN ARE DREAMT OF IN YOUR PHILOSOPHY.

FAIRY

OVER HILL, OVER DALE,
THOROUGH BUSH, THOROUGH BRIER,
OVER PARK, OVER PALE,
THOROUGH FLOOD, THOROUGH FIRE,
I DO WANDER EVERYWHERE,
SWIFTER THAN THE MOON'S SPHERE;
AND I SERVE THE FAIRY QUEEN,
TO DEW HER ORBS UPON THE GREEN.
THE COWSLIPS TALL HER PENSIONERS BE:
IN THEIR GOLD COATS SPOTS YOU SEE;
THOSE BE RUBIES, FAIRY FAVOURS,
IN THOSE FRECKLES LIVE THEIR SAVOURS:
I MUST GO SEEK SOME DEWDROPS HERE
AND HANG A PEARL IN EVERY COWSLIP'S EAR.
FAREWELL, THOU LOB OF SPIRITS; I'LL BE GONE:
OUR QUEEN AND ALL OUR ELVES COME HERE ANON.

ACT II SCENE I

TITANIA

COME, NOW A ROUNDEL AND A FAIRY SONG;

THEN, FOR THE THIRD PART OF A MINUTE, HENCE;

SOME TO KILL CANKERS IN THE MUSK-ROSE BUDS,

SOME WAR WITH RERE-MICE FOR THEIR LEATHERN WINGS,

TO MAKE MY SMALL ELVES COATS, AND SOME KEEP BACK

THE CLAMOROUS OWL THAT NIGHTLY HOOTS AND WONDERS

AT OUR QUAINT SPIRITS. SING ME NOW ASLEEP;

THEN TO YOUR OFFICES AND LET ME REST.

PROSPERO

...THOU, MY SLAVE,

AS THOU REPORT'ST THYSELF, WAST THEN HER SERVANT;

AND, FOR THOU WAST A SPIRIT TOO DELICATE

TO ACT HER EARTHY AND ABHORR'D COMMANDS,

REFUSING HER GRAND HESTS, SHE DID CONFINE THEE,

BY HELP OF HER MORE POTENT MINISTERS

AND IN HER MOST UNMITIGABLE RAGE,

INTO A CLOVEN PINE; WITHIN WHICH RIFT

IMPRISON'D THOU DIDST PAINFULLY REMAIN

A DOZEN YEARS; WITHIN WHICH SPACE SHE DIED

AND LEFT THEE THERE; WHERE THOU DIDST VENT THY GROANS...

...WHAT TORMENT I DID FIND THEE IN; THY GROANS

DID MAKE WOLVES HOWL AND PENETRATE THE BREASTS

OF EVER ANGRY BEARS: IT WAS A TORMENT

TO LAY UPON THE DAMN'D, WHICH SYCORAX

COULD NOT AGAIN UNDO: IT WAS MINE ART,

WHEN I ARRIVED AND HEARD THEE, THAT MADE GAPE

THE PINE AND LET THEE OUT.

ARIEL'S SONG

COME UNTO THESE YELLOW SANDS,
AND THEN TAKE HANDS:
COURTSIED WHEN YOU HAVE AND KISS'D
THE WILD WAVES WHIST,
FOOT IT FEATLY HERE AND THERE;
AND, SWEET SPRITES, THE BURTHEN BEAR.
HARK, HARK!

A MIDSUMMER NIGHT'S DREAM

PUCK

THE KING DOTH KEEP HIS REVELS HERE TONIGHT:
TAKE HEED THE QUEEN COME NOT WITHIN HIS SIGHT;
FOR OBERON IS PASSING FELL AND WROTH,
BECAUSE THAT SHE AS HER ATTENDANT HATH
A LOVELY BOY, STOLEN FROM AN INDIAN KING;
SHE NEVER HAD SO SWEET A CHANGELING;
AND JEALOUS OBERON WOULD HAVE THE CHILD
KNIGHT OF HIS TRAIN, TO TRACE THE FORESTS WILD;
BUT SHE PERFORCE WITHHOLDS THE LOVED BOY,
CROWNS HIM WITH FLOWERS AND MAKES HIM ALL HER JOY:
AND NOW THEY NEVER MEET IN GROVE OR GREEN,
BY FOUNTAIN CLEAR, OR SPANGLED STARLIGHT SHEEN,
BUT, THEY DO SQUARE, THAT ALL THEIR ELVES FOR FEAR
CREEP INTO ACORN-CUPS AND HIDE THEM THERE.

ACT II SCENE I

OBERON

ILL MET BY MOONLIGHT, PROUD TITANIA.

TITANIA

WHAT, JEALOUS OBERON! FAIRIES, SKIP HENCE:
I HAVE FORSWORN HIS BED AND COMPANY.

OBERON

TARRY, RASH WANTON: AM NOT I THY LORD?

TITANIA

THEN I MUST BE THY LADY: BUT I KNOW
WHEN THOU HAST STOLEN AWAY FROM FAIRY LAND,
AND IN THE SHAPE OF CORIN SAT ALL DAY,
PLAYING ON PIPES OF CORN AND VERSING LOVE
TO AMOROUS PHILLIDA. WHY ART THOU HERE,
COME FROM THE FARTHEST STEPPE OF INDIA?
BUT THAT, FORSOOTH, THE BOUNCING AMAZON,
YOUR BUSKIN'D MISTRESS AND YOUR WARRIOR LOVE,
TO THESEUS MUST BE WEDDED, AND YOU COME
TO GIVE THEIR BED JOY AND PROSPERITY.

OBERON

HOW CANST THOU THUS FOR SHAME, TITANIA,

GLANCE AT MY CREDIT WITH HIPPOLYTA,

KNOWING I KNOW THY LOVE TO THESEUS?

DIDST THOU NOT LEAD HIM THROUGH THE GLIMMERING NIGHT

FROM PERIGENIA, WHOM HE RAVISHED?

AND MAKE HIM WITH FAIR AEGLE BREAK HIS FAITH,

WITH ARIADNE AND ANTIOPA?

TITANIA

THESE ARE THE FORGERIES OF JEALOUSY:

AND NEVER, SINCE THE MIDDLE SUMMER'S SPRING,

MET WE ON HILL, IN DALE, FOREST OR MEAD,

BY PAVED FOUNTAIN OR BY RUSHY BROOK,

OR IN THE BEACHED MARGENT OF THE SEA,

TO DANCE OUR RINGLETS TO THE WHISTLING WIND,

BUT WITH THY BRAWLS THOU HAST DISTURB'D OUR SPORT.

TITANIA

SET YOUR HEART AT REST:

THE FAIRY LAND BUYS NOT THE CHILD OF ME.

HIS MOTHER WAS A VOTARESS OF MY ORDER:

AND, IN THE SPICED INDIAN AIR, BY NIGHT,

FULL OFTEN HATH SHE GOSSIP'D BY MY SIDE,

AND SAT WITH ME ON NEPTUNE'S YELLOW SANDS,

MARKING THE EMBARKED TRADERS ON THE FLOOD,

WHEN WE HAVE LAUGH'D TO SEE THE SAILS CONCEIVE

AND GROW BIG-BELLIED WITH THE WANTON WIND;

WHICH SHE, WITH PRETTY AND WITH SWIMMING GAIT

FOLLOWING,--HER WOMB THEN RICH WITH MY YOUNG SQUIRE,--

WOULD IMITATE, AND SAIL UPON THE LAND,

TO FETCH ME TRIFLES, AND RETURN AGAIN,

AS FROM A VOYAGE, RICH WITH MERCHANDISE.

BUT SHE, BEING MORTAL, OF THAT BOY DID DIE;

AND FOR HER SAKE DO I REAR UP HER BOY,

AND FOR HER SAKE I WILL NOT PART WITH HIM.

SECOND WITCH

BY THE PRICKING OF MY THUMBS,
SOMETHING WICKED THIS WAY COMES.
OPEN, LOCKS,
WHOEVER KNOCKS!

MACBETH

HOW NOW, YOU SECRET, BLACK, AND MIDNIGHT HAGS!
WHAT IS'T YOU DO?

ALL

A DEED WITHOUT A NAME.

HAMLET

ANGELS AND MINISTERS OF GRACE DEFEND US!
BE THOU A SPIRIT OF HEALTH OR GOBLIN DAMN'D,
BRING WITH THEE AIRS FROM HEAVEN OR BLASTS FROM HELL,
BE THY INTENTS WICKED OR CHARITABLE,
THOU COMEST IN SUCH A QUESTIONABLE SHAPE
THAT I WILL SPEAK TO THEE

OBERON

... THOU REMEMBEREST
SINCE ONCE I SAT UPON A PROMONTORY,
AND HEARD A MERMAID ON A DOLPHIN'S BACK
UTTERING SUCH DULCET AND HARMONIOUS BREATH
THAT THE RUDE SEA GREW CIVIL AT HER SONG
AND CERTAIN STARS SHOT MADLY FROM THEIR SPHERES,
TO HEAR THE SEA-MAID'S MUSIC.

... THAT VERY TIME I SAW, BUT THOU COULDST NOT,
FLYING BETWEEN THE COLD MOON AND THE EARTH,
CUPID ALL ARM'D: A CERTAIN AIM HE TOOK
AT A FAIR VESTAL THRONED BY THE WEST,
AND LOOSED HIS LOVE-SHAFT SMARTLY FROM HIS BOW,
AS IT SHOULD PIERCE A HUNDRED THOUSAND HEARTS;
BUT I MIGHT SEE YOUNG CUPID'S FIERY SHAFT
QUENCH'D IN THE CHASTE BEAMS OF THE WATERY MOON,
AND THE IMPERIAL VOTARESS PASSED ON,
IN MAIDEN MEDITATION, FANCY-FREE.
YET MARK'D I WHERE THE BOLT OF CUPID FELL:
IT FELL UPON A LITTLE WESTERN FLOWER,
BEFORE MILK-WHITE, NOW PURPLE WITH LOVE'S WOUND,
AND MAIDENS CALL IT LOVE-IN-IDLENESS.
FETCH ME THAT FLOWER; THE HERB I SHEW'D THEE ONCE:
THE JUICE OF IT ON SLEEPING EYE-LIDS LAID
WILL MAKE OR MAN OR WOMAN MADLY DOTE
UPON THE NEXT LIVE CREATURE THAT IT SEES.
FETCH ME THIS HERB; AND BE THOU HERE AGAIN
ERE THE LEVIATHAN CAN SWIM A LEAGUE.

OBERON

WHAT THOU SEEST WHEN THOU DOST WAKE,

DO IT FOR THY TRUE-LOVE TAKE,

LOVE AND LANGUISH FOR HIS SAKE:

BE IT OUNCE, OR CAT, OR BEAR,

PARD, OR BOAR WITH BRISTLED HAIR,

IN THY EYE THAT SHALL APPEAR

WHEN THOU WAKEST, IT IS THY DEAR:

WAKE WHEN SOME VILE THING IS NEAR.

ACT II SCENE II

MERCUTIO

O, THEN, I SEE QUEEN MAB HATH BEEN WITH YOU.

SHE IS THE FAIRIES' MIDWIFE, AND SHE COMES

IN SHAPE NO BIGGER THAN AN AGATE-STONE

ON THE FORE-FINGER OF AN ALDERMAN,

DRAWN WITH A TEAM OF LITTLE ATOMIES

ATHWART MEN'S NOSES AS THEY LIE ASLEEP;

HER WAGON-SPOKES MADE OF LONG SPIDERS' LEGS,

THE COVER OF THE WINGS OF GRASSHOPPERS,

THE TRACES OF THE SMALLEST SPIDER'S WEB,

THE COLLARS OF THE MOONSHINE'S WATERY BEAMS,

HER WHIP OF CRICKET'S BONE, THE LASH OF FILM,

HER WAGONER A SMALL GREY-COATED GNAT,

NOT SO BIG AS A ROUND LITTLE WORM

PRICK'D FROM THE LAZY FINGER OF A MAID;

HER CHARIOT IS AN EMPTY HAZEL-NUT

MADE BY THE JOINER SQUIRREL OR OLD GRUB,

TIME OUT O' MIND THE FAIRIES' COACHMAKERS.

MISTRESS QUICKLY

ABOUT, ABOUT;

SEARCH WINDSOR CASTLE, ELVES, WITHIN AND OUT:

STREW GOOD LUCK, OUPHES, ON EVERY SACRED ROOM:

THAT IT MAY STAND TILL THE PERPETUAL DOOM,

IN STATE AS WHOLESOME AS IN STATE 'TIS FIT,

WORTHY THE OWNER, AND THE OWNER IT.

ACT V SCENE V

OBERON

I PRAY THEE, GIVE IT ME.

I KNOW A BANK WHERE THE WILD THYME BLOWS,

WHERE OXLIPS AND THE NODDING VIOLET GROWS,

QUITE OVER-CANOPIED WITH LUSCIOUS WOODBINE,

WITH SWEET MUSK-ROSES AND WITH EGLANTINE:

THERE SLEEPS TITANIA SOMETIME OF THE NIGHT,

LULL'D IN THESE FLOWERS WITH DANCES AND DELIGHT;

AND THERE THE SNAKE THROWS HER ENAMELL'D SKIN,

WEED WIDE ENOUGH TO WRAP A FAIRY IN:

AND WITH THE JUICE OF THIS I'LL STREAK HER EYES,

AND MAKE HER FULL OF HATEFUL FANTASIES.

ACT II SCENE I

PUCK

I'LL FOLLOW YOU, I'LL LEAD YOU ABOUT A ROUND,
THROUGH BOG, THROUGH BUSH, THROUGH BRAKE, THROUGH BRIER:
SOMETIME A HORSE I'LL BE, SOMETIME A HOUND,
A HOG, A HEADLESS BEAR, SOMETIME A FIRE;
AND NEIGH, AND BARK, AND GRUNT, AND ROAR, AND BURN,

IRIS

YOU NYMPHS, CALL'D NAIADS, OF THE WINDRING BROOKS,
WITH YOUR SEDGED CROWNS AND EVER-HARMLESS LOOKS,
LEAVE YOUR CRISP CHANNELS AND ON THIS GREEN LAND
ANSWER YOUR SUMMONS; JUNO DOES COMMAND:
COME, TEMPERATE NYMPHS, AND HELP TO CELEBRATE
A CONTRACT OF TRUE LOVE; BE NOT TOO LATE.

ACT IV SCENE I

THE TEMPEST

PROSPERO

YE ELVES OF HILLS, BROOKS, STANDING LAKES AND GROVES,
AND YE THAT ON THE SANDS WITH PRINTLESS FOOT
DO CHASE THE EBBING NEPTUNE AND DO FLY HIM
WHEN HE COMES BACK; YOU DEMI-PUPPETS THAT
BY MOONSHINE DO THE GREEN SOUR RINGLETS MAKE,
WHEREOF THE EWE NOT BITES, AND YOU WHOSE PASTIME
IS TO MAKE MIDNIGHT MUSHROOMS, THAT REJOICE
TO HEAR THE SOLEMN CURFEW; BY WHOSE AID,
WEAK MASTERS THOUGH YE BE, I HAVE BEDIMM'D
THE NOONTIDE SUN, CALL'D FORTH THE MUTINOUS WINDS,
AND 'TWIXT THE GREEN SEA AND THE AZURED VAULT
SET ROARING WAR: TO THE DREAD RATTLING THUNDER
HAVE I GIVEN FIRE AND RIFTED JOVE'S STOUT OAK
WITH HIS OWN BOLT; THE STRONG-BASED PROMONTORY
HAVE I MADE SHAKE AND BY THE SPURS PLUCK'D UP
THE PINE AND CEDAR: GRAVES AT MY COMMAND
HAVE WAKED THEIR SLEEPERS, OPED, AND LET 'EM FORTH
BY MY SO POTENT ART. BUT THIS ROUGH MAGIC
I HERE ABJURE, AND, WHEN I HAVE REQUIRED
SOME HEAVENLY MUSIC, WHICH EVEN NOW I DO,
TO WORK MINE END UPON THEIR SENSES THAT
THIS AIRY CHARM IS FOR, I'LL BREAK MY STAFF,
BURY IT CERTAIN FATHOMS IN THE EARTH,
AND DEEPER THAN DID EVER PLUMMET SOUND
I'LL DROWN MY BOOK.

TITANIA

OUT OF THIS WOOD DO NOT DESIRE TO GO:

THOU SHALT REMAIN HERE, WHETHER THOU WILT OR NO.

I AM A SPIRIT OF NO COMMON RATE;

THE SUMMER STILL DOTH TEND UPON MY STATE;

AND I DO LOVE THEE: THEREFORE, GO WITH ME;

I'LL GIVE THEE FAIRIES TO ATTEND ON THEE,

AND THEY SHALL FETCH THEE JEWELS FROM THE DEEP,

AND SING WHILE THOU ON PRESSED FLOWERS DOST

SLEEP;

AND I WILL PURGE THY MORTAL GROSSNESS SO

THAT THOU SHALT LIKE AN AIRY SPIRIT GO.

PEASEBLOSSOM! COBWEB! MOTH! AND MUSTARDSEED!

TITANIA

BE KIND AND COURTEOUS TO THIS GENTLEMAN;
HOP IN HIS WALKS AND GAMBOL IN HIS EYES;
FEED HIM WITH APRICOCKS AND DEWBERRIES,
WITH PURPLE GRAPES, GREEN FIGS, AND MULBERRIES;
THE HONEY-BAGS STEAL FROM THE HUMBLE-BEES,
AND FOR NIGHT-TAPERS CROP THEIR WAXEN THIGHS
AND LIGHT THEM AT THE FIERY GLOW-WORM'S EYES,
TO HAVE MY LOVE TO BED AND TO ARISE;
AND PLUCK THE WINGS FROM PAINTED BUTTERFLIES
TO FAN THE MOONBEAMS FROM HIS SLEEPING EYES:
NOD TO HIM, ELVES, AND DO HIM COURTESIES.

ACT III SCENE I

MACBETH

FIRST WITCH

ROUND ABOUT THE CAULDRON GO;

IN THE POISON'D ENTRAILS THROW.

TOAD, THAT UNDER COLD STONE

DAYS AND NIGHTS HAS THIRTY-ONE

SWELTER'D VENOM SLEEPING GOT,

BOIL THOU FIRST I' THE CHARMED POT.

ALL

DOUBLE, DOUBLE TOIL AND TROUBLE;

FIRE BURN, AND CAULDRON BUBBLE.

SECOND WITCH

FILLET OF A FENNY SNAKE,

IN THE CAULDRON BOIL AND BAKE;

EYE OF NEWT AND TOE OF FROG,

WOOL OF BAT AND TONGUE OF DOG,

ADDER'S FORK AND BLIND-WORM'S STING,

LIZARD'S LEG AND OWLET'S WING,

FOR A CHARM OF POWERFUL TROUBLE,

LIKE A HELL-BROTH BOIL AND BUBBLE.

ALL

DOUBLE, DOUBLE TOIL AND TROUBLE;

FIRE BURN AND CAULDRON BUBBLE.

BRUTUS

HOW ILL THIS TAPER BURNS! HA! WHO COMES HERE?
I THINK IT IS THE WEAKNESS OF MINE EYES
THAT SHAPES THIS MONSTROUS APPARITION.
IT COMES UPON ME. ART THOU ANY THING?
ART THOU SOME GOD, SOME ANGEL, OR SOME DEVIL,
THAT MAKEST MY BLOOD COLD AND MY HAIR TO STARE?
SPEAK TO ME WHAT THOU ART.

GHOST

THY EVIL SPIRIT, BRUTUS.

OBERON

. . .I WILL RELEASE THE FAIRY QUEEN.
BE AS THOU WAST WONT TO BE;
SEE AS THOU WAST WONT TO SEE:
DIAN'S BUD O'ER CUPID'S FLOWER
HATH SUCH FORCE AND BLESSED POWER.
NOW, MY TITANIA; WAKE YOU, MY SWEET QUEEN.

TITANIA

MY OBERON! WHAT VISIONS HAVE I SEEN!
METHOUGHT I WAS ENAMOUR'D OF AN ASS.

OBERON

THERE LIES YOUR LOVE.

A MIDSUMMER NIGHT'S DREAM

PUCK

NOW THE HUNGRY LION ROARS,

AND THE WOLF BEHOWLS THE MOON;

WHILST THE HEAVY PLOUGHMAN SNORES,

ALL WITH WEARY TASK FORDONE.

NOW THE WASTED BRANDS DO GLOW,

WHILST THE SCREECH-OWL, SCREECHING LOUD,

PUTS THE WRETCH THAT LIES IN WOE

IN REMEMBRANCE OF A SHROUD.

NOW IT IS THE TIME OF NIGHT

THAT THE GRAVES ALL GAPING WIDE,

EVERY ONE LETS FORTH HIS SPRITE,

IN THE CHURCH-WAY PATHS TO GLIDE:

AND WE FAIRIES, THAT DO RUN

BY THE TRIPLE HECATE'S TEAM,

FROM THE PRESENCE OF THE SUN,

FOLLOWING DARKNESS LIKE A DREAM,

NOW ARE FROLIC: NOT A MOUSE

SHALL DISTURB THIS HALLOW'D HOUSE:

I AM SENT WITH BROOM BEFORE,

TO SWEEP THE DUST BEHIND THE DOOR.

MISTRESS QUICKLY

AND NIGHTLY, MEADOW-FAIRIES, LOOK YOU SING,

LIKE TO THE GARTER'S COMPASS, IN A RING:

THE EXPRESSURE THAT IT BEARS, GREEN LET IT BE,

MORE FERTILE-FRESH THAN ALL THE FIELD TO SEE;

AND 'HONI SOIT QUI MAL Y PENSE' WRITE

IN EMERALD TUFTS, FLOWERS PURPLE, BLUE AND WHITE;

LET SAPPHIRE, PEARL AND RICH EMBROIDERY,

BUCKLED BELOW FAIR KNIGHTHOOD'S BENDING KNEE:

FAIRIES USE FLOWERS FOR THEIR CHARACTERY.

FIRST WITCH

WHY, HOW NOW, HECATE! YOU LOOK ANGERLY.

HECATE

HAVE I NOT REASON, BELDAMS AS YOU ARE,
SAUCY AND OVERBOLD? HOW DID YOU DARE
TO TRADE AND TRAFFIC WITH MACBETH
IN RIDDLES AND AFFAIRS OF DEATH;
AND I, THE MISTRESS OF YOUR CHARMS,
THE CLOSE CONTRIVER OF ALL HARMS,
WAS NEVER CALL'D TO BEAR MY PART,
OR SHOW THE GLORY OF OUR ART?

OBERON

THROUGH THE HOUSE GIVE GATHERING LIGHT,

BY THE DEAD AND DROWSY FIRE:

EVERY ELF AND FAIRY SPRITE

HOP AS LIGHT AS BIRD FROM BRIER;

AND THIS DITTY, AFTER ME,

SING, AND DANCE IT TRIPPINGLY.

TITANIA

FIRST, REHEARSE YOUR SONG BY ROTE

TO EACH WORD A WARBLING NOTE:

HAND IN HAND, WITH FAIRY GRACE,

WILL WE SING, AND BLESS THIS PLACE.

A MIDSUMMER NIGHT'S DREAM

THESEUS

MORE STRANGE THAN TRUE: I NEVER MAY BELIEVE
THESE ANTIQUE FABLES, NOR THESE FAIRY TOYS.
LOVERS AND MADMEN HAVE SUCH SEETHING BRAINS,
SUCH SHAPING FANTASIES, THAT APPREHEND
MORE THAN COOL REASON EVER COMPREHENDS.
THE LUNATIC, THE LOVER AND THE POET
ARE OF IMAGINATION ALL COMPACT:
ONE SEES MORE DEVILS THAN VAST HELL CAN HOLD,
THAT IS, THE MADMAN: THE LOVER, ALL AS FRANTIC,
SEES HELEN'S BEAUTY IN A BROW OF EGYPT:
THE POET'S EYE, IN FINE FRENZY ROLLING,
DOTH GLANCE FROM HEAVEN TO EARTH, FROM EARTH TO HEAVEN;
AND AS IMAGINATION BODIES FORTH
THE FORMS OF THINGS UNKNOWN, THE POET'S PEN
TURNS THEM TO SHAPES AND GIVES TO AIRY NOTHING
A LOCAL HABITATION AND A NAME.
SUCH TRICKS HATH STRONG IMAGINATION,
THAT IF IT WOULD BUT APPREHEND SOME JOY,
IT COMPREHENDS SOME BRINGER OF THAT JOY;
OR IN THE NIGHT, IMAGINING SOME FEAR,
HOW EASY IS A BUSH SUPPOSED A BEAR!

HIPPOLYTA

BUT ALL THE STORY OF THE NIGHT TOLD OVER,
AND ALL THEIR MINDS TRANSFIGURED SO TOGETHER,
MORE WITNESSETH THAN FANCY'S IMAGES
AND GROWS TO SOMETHING OF GREAT CONSTANCY;
BUT, HOWSOEVER, STRANGE AND ADMIRABLE.

PROSPERO

NOW MY CHARMS ARE ALL O'ERTHROWN,
AND WHAT STRENGTH I HAVE'S MINE OWN,
WHICH IS MOST FAINT

ARIEL SINGS

WHERE THE BEE SUCKS. THERE SUCK I:
IN A COWSLIP'S BELL I LIE;
THERE I COUCH WHEN OWLS DO CRY.
ON THE BAT'S BACK I DO FLY
AFTER SUMMER MERRILY.
MERRILY, MERRILY SHALL I LIVE NOW
UNDER THE BLOSSOM THAT HANGS ON THE BOUGH.

ACT V SCENE I

FALSTAFF

THEY ARE FAIRIES; HE THAT SPEAKS TO THEM SHALL DIE:
I'LL WINK AND COUCH: NO MAN THEIR WORKS MUST EYE.

ACT V SCENE V

PROSPERO

OUR REVELS NOW ARE ENDED. THESE OUR ACTORS,
AS I FORETOLD YOU, WERE ALL SPIRITS AND
ARE MELTED INTO AIR, INTO THIN AIR:
AND, LIKE THE BASELESS FABRIC OF THIS VISION,
THE CLOUD-CAPP'D TOWERS, THE GORGEOUS PALACES,
THE SOLEMN TEMPLES, THE GREAT GLOBE ITSELF,
YE ALL WHICH IT INHERIT, SHALL DISSOLVE
AND, LIKE THIS INSUBSTANTIAL PAGEANT FADED,
LEAVE NOT A RACK BEHIND. WE ARE SUCH STUFF
AS DREAMS ARE MADE ON, AND OUR LITTLE LIFE
IS ROUNDED WITH A SLEEP.

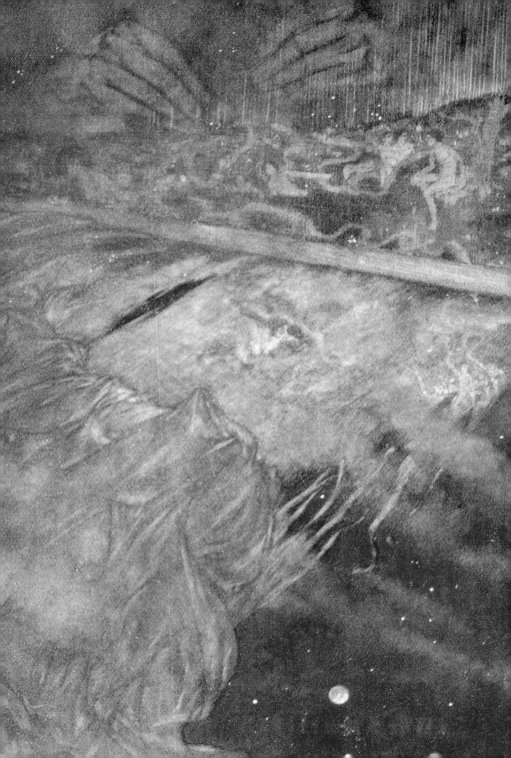

PUCK

IF WE SHADOWS HAVE OFFENDED,
THINK BUT THIS, AND ALL IS MENDED,
THAT YOU HAVE BUT SLUMBER'D HERE
WHILE THESE VISIONS DID APPEAR.

PICTURE CREDITS

PICTURE CREDITS

COLOPHON

THIS BOOK WAS TYPESET IN CENTAUR & BICKHAM SCRIPT

BOOK & COVER DESIGN BY SACHEVERELL DARLING & MIKE HARRISON
AT BLUE LANTERN STUDIO

PRINTED & BOUND IN SINGAPORE